# MY WORRY BOOK

## FOR KIDS

THESE THOUGHTS BELONG TO

# WHAT'S IN MY WORRY BOOK?

**1** The first part of this book is all about your worries. Your place to let it all out! Write down your worries, anxieties, fears, and stresses. Don't hold back!

**2** Next you'll find a place to keep track of how to cope with worries when they come up.

**3** The last part of this book is for you to use whenever you feel the worries coming on. Draw, write, color. Get it down on paper and out of your head.

· · · · · · · · ·

# HOW DO I USE THIS BOOK?

This book is all about YOU. Your thoughts and your feelings. Take it out whenever need to. This book is always here for you - no matter day or night.

Write, color, draw, scribble, doodle, and scratch out. Anything goes in your worry book.

_____

_____

_____

_____

_____

_____

_____

_____

_____

_____

_____

_____

_____

_____

_____

_____

_____

_____

_____

_____

_____

_____

# DAYTIME WORRIES

_____
_____
_____
_____
_____
_____
_____
_____
_____
_____

# NIGHTTIME WORRIES

_____
_____
_____
_____
_____
_____
_____
_____
_____
_____

# THOUGHTS I'M THINKING

# Feels I'm Feeling

Places I feel
# SCARED

_____

_____

_____

_____

_____

_____

_____

_____

_____

_____

_____

Things that make me

# ANXIOUS

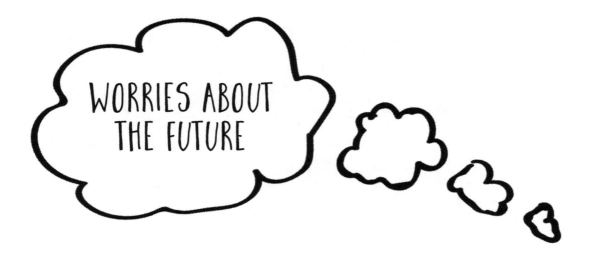

WORRIES ABOUT THE FUTURE

WORRIES ABOUT THE PAST

## WHERE I FEEL SAFE

_____

_____

_____

_____

_____

# I FEEL BETTER WHEN...

_____

_____

_____

_____

_____

_____

_____

_____

# MY COPING STRATEGIES

BEFORE ∿∿∿∿

_____

_____

_____

_____

>>>>>>>>>>> DURING <<<<<<<<<<<<

_____

_____

_____

_____

ℓℓℓℓℓℓℓℓℓℓℓℓ AFTER

_____

_____

_____

_____

# ◇◇◇◇◇◇ OTHER IMPORTANT STUFF ◇◇◇◇◇◇

◇ ◇ ◇ ◇ ◇ ◇ SOMETHING I WANT TO SAY ◇ ◇ ◇ ◇ ◇ ◇ ◇

## WHAT IS HAPPENING?

TODAY IS

_____

_____

_____

_____

NOT BAD ①②③④⑤⑥⑦⑧⑨⑩ WORST EVER

## HOW AM I RESPONDING?

| MY BREATH | MY HEART | MY BODY |
|---|---|---|
| | | |

## MY THOUGHTS

_____

_____

_____

_____

_____

## MY FEELINGS

_____

_____

_____

_____

_____

# WHAT IS HAPPENING?

_____

_____

_____

_____

NOT BAD ①─②─③─④─⑤─⑥─⑦─⑧─⑨─⑩ WORST EVER

## HOW AM I RESPONDING?

| MY BREATH | MY HEART | MY BODY |
|---|---|---|
|  |  |  |

## MY THOUGHTS

_____

_____

_____

_____

_____

## MY FEELINGS

_____

_____

_____

_____

_____

## WHAT IS HAPPENING?

TODAY IS

_____

_____

_____

_____

NOT BAD ① ② ③ ④ ⑤ ⑥ ⑦ ⑧ ⑨ ⑩ WORST EVER

## HOW AM I RESPONDING?

| MY BREATH | MY HEART | MY BODY |
|-----------|----------|---------|
|           |          |         |

## MY THOUGHTS

_____

_____

_____

_____

_____

## MY FEELINGS

_____

_____

_____

_____

_____

# WHAT IS HAPPENING?

TODAY IS

NOT BAD ①─②─③─④─⑤─⑥─⑦─⑧─⑨─⑩ WORST EVER

## HOW AM I RESPONDING?

| MY BREATH | MY HEART | MY BODY |
| --- | --- | --- |
| | | |

## MY THOUGHTS

## MY FEELINGS

# WHAT IS HAPPENING?

TODAY IS

_____

_____

_____

_____

NOT BAD ① ② ③ ④ ⑤ ⑥ ⑦ ⑧ ⑨ ⑩ WORST EVER

## HOW AM I RESPONDING?

| MY BREATH | MY HEART | MY BODY |
|---|---|---|
|  |  |  |

## MY THOUGHTS

_____

_____

_____

_____

_____

## MY FEELINGS

_____

_____

_____

_____

_____

# WHAT IS HAPPENING?

TODAY IS

_____

_____

_____

_____

NOT BAD ①─②─③─④─⑤─⑥─⑦─⑧─⑨─⑩ WORST EVER

## HOW AM I RESPONDING?

| MY BREATH | MY HEART | MY BODY |
| --- | --- | --- |
| | | |

## MY THOUGHTS

_____

_____

_____

_____

_____

## MY FEELINGS

_____

_____

_____

_____

_____

## WHAT IS HAPPENING?

TODAY IS

_____

_____

_____

_____

NOT BAD ①②③④⑤⑥⑦⑧⑨⑩ WORST EVER

## HOW AM I RESPONDING?

| MY BREATH | MY HEART | MY BODY |
|---|---|---|
|  |  |  |

## MY THOUGHTS

_____

_____

_____

_____

_____

## MY FEELINGS

_____

_____

_____

_____

_____

# WHAT IS HAPPENING?

TODAY IS

_____

_____

_____

NOT BAD ①—②—③—④—⑤—⑥—⑦—⑧—⑨—⑩ WORST EVER

## HOW AM I RESPONDING?

| MY BREATH | MY HEART | MY BODY |
|---|---|---|
| | | |

### MY THOUGHTS

_____

_____

_____

_____

_____

### MY FEELINGS

_____

_____

_____

_____

_____

# WHAT IS HAPPENING?

_____

_____

_____

_____

NOT BAD ─(1)─(2)─(3)─(4)─(5)─(6)─(7)─(8)─(9)─(10)─ WORST EVER

## HOW AM I RESPONDING?

| MY BREATH | MY HEART | MY BODY |
|---|---|---|
| | | |

## MY THOUGHTS

_____

_____

_____

_____

_____

## MY FEELINGS

_____

_____

_____

_____

_____

# WHAT IS HAPPENING?

_____

_____

_____

_____

NOT BAD ①—②—③—④—⑤—⑥—⑦—⑧—⑨—⑩ WORST EVER

## HOW AM I RESPONDING?

| MY BREATH | MY HEART | MY BODY |
|---|---|---|
| | | |

## MY THOUGHTS

_____

_____

_____

_____

_____

## MY FEELINGS

_____

_____

_____

_____

_____

# WHAT IS HAPPENING?

TODAY IS

_____

_____

_____

_____

NOT BAD  ①②③④⑤⑥⑦⑧⑨⑩  WORST EVER

## HOW AM I RESPONDING?

| MY BREATH | MY HEART | MY BODY |
|---|---|---|
|  |  |  |

## MY THOUGHTS

_____

_____

_____

_____

_____

_____

## MY FEELINGS

_____

_____

_____

_____

_____

_____

# WHAT IS HAPPENING?

TODAY IS

_____
_____
_____
_____

NOT BAD ①②③④⑤⑥⑦⑧⑨⑩ WORST EVER

## HOW AM I RESPONDING?

| MY BREATH | MY HEART | MY BODY |
|---|---|---|
| | | |

### MY THOUGHTS

_____
_____
_____
_____
_____
_____

### MY FEELINGS

_____
_____
_____
_____
_____
_____

# WHAT IS HAPPENING?

TODAY IS

_____

_____

_____

_____

NOT BAD ①②③④⑤⑥⑦⑧⑨⑩ WORST EVER

## HOW AM I RESPONDING?

| MY BREATH | MY HEART | MY BODY |
|-----------|----------|---------|
|           |          |         |

## MY THOUGHTS

_____

_____

_____

_____

_____

_____

## MY FEELINGS

_____

_____

_____

_____

_____

_____

# WHAT IS HAPPENING?

TODAY IS

_____

_____

_____

_____

NOT BAD  ①—②—③—④—⑤—⑥—⑦—⑧—⑨—⑩  WORST EVER

## HOW AM I RESPONDING?

| MY BREATH | MY HEART | MY BODY |
|---|---|---|
|  |  |  |

## MY THOUGHTS

_____

_____

_____

_____

_____

## MY FEELINGS

_____

_____

_____

_____

_____

# WHAT IS HAPPENING?

_____

_____

_____

_____

NOT BAD ① ② ③ ④ ⑤ ⑥ ⑦ ⑧ ⑨ ⑩ WORST EVER

## HOW AM I RESPONDING?

| MY BREATH | MY HEART | MY BODY |
|---|---|---|
|  |  |  |

## MY THOUGHTS

_____

_____

_____

_____

_____

_____

## MY FEELINGS

_____

_____

_____

_____

_____

_____

# WHAT IS HAPPENING?

TODAY IS

_____

_____

_____

_____

NOT BAD ① ② ③ ④ ⑤ ⑥ ⑦ ⑧ ⑨ ⑩ WORST EVER

## HOW AM I RESPONDING?

| MY BREATH | MY HEART | MY BODY |
|---|---|---|
| | | |

## MY THOUGHTS

_____

_____

_____

_____

_____

## MY FEELINGS

_____

_____

_____

_____

_____

# WHAT IS HAPPENING?

TODAY IS

_____
_____
_____
_____

NOT BAD ①②③④⑤⑥⑦⑧⑨⑩ WORST EVER

## HOW AM I RESPONDING?

| MY BREATH | MY HEART | MY BODY |
| --- | --- | --- |
| | | |

## MY THOUGHTS

_____
_____
_____
_____
_____
_____

## MY FEELINGS

_____
_____
_____
_____
_____
_____

# WHAT IS HAPPENING?

TODAY IS

_____

_____

_____

_____

NOT BAD ①—②—③—④—⑤—⑥—⑦—⑧—⑨—⑩ WORST EVER

## HOW AM I RESPONDING?

| MY BREATH | MY HEART | MY BODY |
|---|---|---|
|  |  |  |

## MY THOUGHTS

_____

_____

_____

_____

_____

## MY FEELINGS

_____

_____

_____

_____

_____

# WHAT IS HAPPENING?

TODAY IS

_____

_____

_____

_____

NOT BAD ① ② ③ ④ ⑤ ⑥ ⑦ ⑧ ⑨ ⑩ WORST EVER

## HOW AM I RESPONDING?

| MY BREATH | MY HEART | MY BODY |
|---|---|---|
|  |  |  |

## MY THOUGHTS

_____

_____

_____

_____

_____

## MY FEELINGS

_____

_____

_____

_____

_____

# WHAT IS HAPPENING?

TODAY IS

_____

_____

_____

_____

NOT BAD ①―②―③―④―⑤―⑥―⑦―⑧―⑨―⑩ WORST EVER

## HOW AM I RESPONDING?

| MY BREATH | MY HEART | MY BODY |
|-----------|----------|---------|
|           |          |         |

## MY THOUGHTS

_____

_____

_____

_____

_____

## MY FEELINGS

_____

_____

_____

_____

_____

# WHAT IS HAPPENING?

_____

_____

_____

_____

NOT BAD ──（1）─（2）─（3）─（4）─（5）─（6）─（7）─（8）─（9）─（10）── WORST EVER

## HOW AM I RESPONDING?

| MY BREATH | MY HEART | MY BODY |
|---|---|---|
|  |  |  |

## MY THOUGHTS

_____

_____

_____

_____

_____

_____

## MY FEELINGS

_____

_____

_____

_____

_____

_____

# WHAT IS HAPPENING?

TODAY IS

_____

_____

_____

NOT BAD ①—②—③—④—⑤—⑥—⑦—⑧—⑨—⑩ WORST EVER

## HOW AM I RESPONDING?

| MY BREATH | MY HEART | MY BODY |
|---|---|---|
|  |  |  |

### MY THOUGHTS

_____

_____

_____

_____

_____

### MY FEELINGS

_____

_____

_____

_____

_____

# WHAT IS HAPPENING?

TODAY IS

_____
_____
_____
_____

NOT BAD ①—②—③—④—⑤—⑥—⑦—⑧—⑨—⑩ WORST EVER

## HOW AM I RESPONDING?

| MY BREATH | MY HEART | MY BODY |
|---|---|---|
|  |  |  |

## MY THOUGHTS

_____
_____
_____
_____
_____
_____

## MY FEELINGS

_____
_____
_____
_____
_____
_____

# WHAT IS HAPPENING?

TODAY IS

_____

_____

_____

_____

NOT BAD ①②③④⑤⑥⑦⑧⑨⑩ WORST EVER

## HOW AM I RESPONDING?

| MY BREATH | MY HEART | MY BODY |
|---|---|---|
| | | |

## MY THOUGHTS

_____

_____

_____

_____

_____

## MY FEELINGS

_____

_____

_____

_____

_____

# WHAT IS HAPPENING?

TODAY IS

_____

_____

_____

_____

NOT BAD ① ② ③ ④ ⑤ ⑥ ⑦ ⑧ ⑨ ⑩ WORST EVER

## HOW AM I RESPONDING?

| MY BREATH | MY HEART | MY BODY |
|---|---|---|
|  |  |  |

## MY THOUGHTS

_____

_____

_____

_____

_____

_____

## MY FEELINGS

_____

_____

_____

_____

_____

_____

Made in the USA
Columbia, SC
07 February 2021

32494413R00039